Mother to Daughter

Shared Wisdom from the Heart

by Melissa Harrison and
Harry H. Harrison, Jr.

Workman Publishing Company

New York

Library of Congress Cataloging-in-Publication Data
Harrison, Harry H.
Mother to daughter : life lessons to pass on / by Harry H. Harrison, Jr. and Melissa Harrison.
p. cm.
ISBN 978-0-7611-3792-4

1. Mothers and daughters. 2. Parenting. 3. Motherhood. I. Harrison, Melissa, 1951– II. Title.
HQ755.85.H3745 2005
306.874'3—dc22   2004065935

Workman books are available at special discounts when purchased in bulk for
premiums and sales promotions as well as for fund-raising or educational use.
Special editions or book excerpts can be created to specification.
For details, contact the Special Sales Director at the address below.

Workman Publishing Company, Inc.
225 Varick Street
New York, NY 10014-4381
www.workman.com

Cover and book design by Paul Gamarello
Cover photograph by Julie Gang

First printing: February 2005
10 9 8 7 6

To Sara & Wrenna

Mother to Daughter

From Gramma, Mary
12/3/14

Acknowledgments

This book was the combined effort of a number of remarkable women who shared stories of their mothers, daughters, and grandmothers. Special thanks go to Rosalie Mayo and Sweet Hopkins, who went above and beyond to help recruit women for this project. And the ladies in the "Bee" revealed the power of a group of women who love one another and stand by each other without even a hint of jealousy.

Gigi Berry	Sweet Hopkins	Jordan Murphy
Angela Bibb	Robbie Johnson	Susan Newberry
Judy Birkes	Sharon Johnson	Eileen Oden
Trish Bittle	Theresa Kainer	Lynn O'Shea
Steph Brinlee	Carole Kaney-Francis	Claire Parker
LaShaw Christen	Kathy King	Lisa Rees
Dena Compton	Jean Klinger	Suzanne Scott
Julianne Drost	Laurie Kohl	Christine Somers
Erika Everett	Cathy Krejci	Sara Sowan
Carol Flores	Amy Krupka	Martha Stammer
Susan Hood	Nancy McCord	Brooke Sullivan
Ivy Hopkins	Stephanie Methvin	Melissa Trycha
Kendal Hopkins	Jeannette Miesse	Tatum Tuthill

Preface

....

"It is a mystical relationship."
—Gigi

There have been ten jillion books about how to repair the mother-daughter relationship.

Precious few about building it.

This is what *Mother to Daughter* is about.

A mother's relationship with her daughter starts before the beginning; in fact, it starts in the mother's own childhood. Because the childhood she has determines the childhood she'll give her own daughter.

A mother teaches her daughter how to feel about herself, about handling pressure, about relishing life's joys and conquering fears. She teaches her daughter how to act like a lady, when to turn on the charm, how to dress up, the importance of trusting God, and how to care for a daughter of her own someday. She teaches her daughter everything she knows about being a woman, then gets frustrated beyond belief when she acts like one.

As one mom said, "Raising a daughter is like growing a flower. You give it your best. If you've done your job well, she blooms. And right after that, she leaves."

All moms instinctively know this. Maybe loving someone so much, someone that is such a part of you, is what makes the mother-daughter relationship so special. Mothers know that love is forever. And that's a lesson their daughters can't wait to pass along.

For more parenting insights, visit www.raisingparents.com.

The Five Keys

1. Be her mother. Not her best friend.
2. Let her live her own dreams. Don't try to make her live yours.
3. Be a strong, confident woman.
4. Be a good wife. You're shaping her future relationships with men.
5. Be aware that your goal is not to be the center of her life forever, but to work yourself out of a job.

The Bonding
Years

Get ready for the most intimate, explosive, loving relationship you'll ever have. Except for the one you had with your mom.

Start now to be the kind of mother you always wanted to be. Don't wait until she's eighteen.

Accept the fact that
she is Daddy's little girl.
She knows this
in the cradle already.

Realize you may not be able to imagine leaving her and going back to work. That's perfectly okay.

Realize it's normal to check on her fifty times a night in the beginning.

Forget that you used to be cool and sexy. Nowadays, you won't leave the house without a stroller, a backpack, a child's seat, diaper changes, snacks, stuffed animals, and something to disinfect your hands.

Early on, raise her
to be adventurous.

Remember, successfully changing
a little girl's diaper means:
1. Nothing hits you in the face.
2. Your clothes remain clean.
3. Your sense of smell still
   functions.

Keep in mind that all she wants to be doing—for the greatest part of her young life—is what you're doing.

Know the names of her
dolls and stuffed animals.
Ask her to tell you stories
about them.

Play tickle monster
with her.

Making her laugh will be your primary occupation. Hard-nosed investment bankers have been known to make weird faces and crazy sounds in the most public places just to be rewarded with a smile.

Be prepared.
Little girls' emotions
surprise even their
mothers.

Start off her baking career by letting her sprinkle the holiday cookies with sugar and sprinkles. She'll love it. She might even hit a cookie or two.

Realize that as a mom your job is to decipher if she's crying because something is wrong or if she just wants attention. Men have never figured it out.

Help her memorize her
full name and address.
This is more important
than the ABC's.

Agree to let her brush and style your hair. And Dad's hair. This will pass in a couple of years.

Learn the songs
she sings at school and
sing them together.

Just accept that while you may have saved all your Barbie dolls for this very moment, she may play with them for . . . ten minutes.

Introduce her to the joys of a lawn sprinkler in the summertime. Little girls love to splash around.

Start saving for dance lessons.
And piano.
And gymnastics.
And swimming.
And cheerleading.

Remember, the traditions you establish now will be passed on to her daughter.

Don't feel guilty
when you absolutely
need a little space.
Just get a sitter.

Make her tea parties special events—invite all the teddy bears in the house, "eat" the cookies she hands you, pour milk and put sugar in your cup, go the whole nine yards.

Have a skipping contest.
This is especially handy
when you need to get
somewhere fast.

Never let her question
that you love her
unconditionally.

Display her artwork as
carefully as you display
your other paintings.

Resolve not to do anything for her that she can do for herself. This will serve the two of you well.

Read to her every night—
classics from your childhood,
as well as her own favorites.

Watch how she talks to
her dolls. You'll learn
how you're talking to her.

Teach her to be a little
kinder than necessary.

Enjoy the moment.
Breathe. Show her that
a mom can sit down
on the floor and relax.

Check little brothers
and pets regularly for
glued-on sequins and
stars, glitter, or lipstick.

Tell her she can be anything she wants. But then don't ask her why in the world she wants to be an actress or doctor or soldier or housewife.

Put little love notes
in her lunch box.
Draw pictures
if she can't read.

Watch what her
babysitters wear
around her. Older girls
are her role models.

Cherish the days when
she looks up and says,
"I love you."

Show her that even at the age of four an especially difficult day can be made better with a bubble bath.

Don't be afraid that an unhappy
relationship with your mother
means you'll have one with your
daughter. If anything, you know
the mistakes.

Crank up the stereo and show her how to boogie.

Let her fall down.
Let her pick herself back up again.
Let her develop determination.

Realize that she'll know when it's time for the training wheels to come off. (This will be true pretty much her whole life.)

Don't think doing everything right will eliminate confrontations, tears, accusations, and emotional outbursts. In fact, these often mean you *are* doing everything right.

Buy her "boy" toys too, like
chemistry sets, building blocks,
miniature cars, and baseball gloves.

Make dinnertime sacred.
Everyone is to attend,
everyone will be heard.

Pop a big bowl of
popcorn, sit down with
her, and watch Cinderella
for the 63rd time.

Share stories of your mother and grandmothers with her. Remember, girls are keepers of the flame.

Let her pick out fabric,
and sew doll clothes together.
If you can't sew, then help her
make paper doll clothes!

Don't go overboard
on praise. Be specific
or it will stop meaning
anything.

Give her a garden row all her own, where she can plant sunflowers or pumpkins or cherry tomatoes. Her biggest thrill will be eating something that she grew herself.

You'll always be
surprised by her stages.
Even though you went
through them too.

Go on a picnic together,
just the two of you.
Even if it's in your backyard.

Introduce her to the
wonder and joys of
the library.

Make ice cream sundaes
together. Frozen yogurt
is an acceptable substitute;
hot fudge is irreplaceable.

Put together a huge box of dress-up clothing, with different hats and cowgirl gear and princess "jewelry" for her to play with. She (and her friends) will love this.

If her father ever says
she's fat, whack him.

Teach her how to climb a tree (and climb back down), to swing across the monkey bars, to throw a punch. Let her learn she's strong.

Write poems together
and preserve them.
You'll both love reading your
poetry years from now.

She'll be hearing about the dangers of alcohol and drugs as soon as school begins. She needs to hear it from you too.

Take her to the ocean.
It will be magic.

Let her smear her face with your lipstick, put on your earrings, and stagger around in your high heels. But remind her, no wearing makeup out of the house until you say so.

Teach her manners early.
And enforce them,
even when she's thirteen.

Send her picture
postcards when you're
out of town.

Teach her to see the world with fresh eyes every morning.

Let her play with your computer, and she'll never be intimidated by it.

Teach her to pick up
after herself. This will
serve her well the rest
of her life.

Take her to work with you once
in a while so she can see what you
do. (Let her help you and she'll
feel *very* important.)

Keep in mind that she's always watching you: how you care for your family, how you worship, how you handle life.

Keep a journal about her. Give it to her when she's eighteen.

Never make her
feel responsible
for your anger.
Unless she is responsible.

.

Praise her for her abilities
and accomplishments,
not her looks.

Don't think that just because school starts your life will slow down. PTA beckons.

Remember, the secret to having deep, candid conversations with her as a teenager is to start having those conversations with her now.

Realize that most girls' strength is reading and verbal communication. But introduce her to puzzles and brain-teasers and strategy games like chess as well.

Post a rule:
No whining.

When she's about seven years old, she'll start noticing what people *have*. Teach her to pay more attention to what people *are*.

Prepare her for the peer pressure she's going to face in school. It can start insanely early.

Don't buy the message that eight-year-olds should have their tummies exposed, thighs revealed, and lips glossed.

Start her skiing or snowboarding early. She'll soon be able to dust the boys.

Remember, little girls
can get so obsessed with the
concept of "fairness,"
they have twenty-four-hour
calculators going in their heads.

Realize that she won't battle you for the phone until she's ten. Then it's every woman for herself.

Buy her a diary.
With a lock and key.

Realize that one of your most important jobs is to give her a sense of self . . . to help her define who she is, so no one else will.

Remember to tell
her she's beautiful.
Inside and out.

Post her spelling words on the refrigerator door. Use them in conversation.

Make fruit-topped, Mickey Mouse–shaped pancakes together. Whipped cream and batter and fruit will go everywhere. She'll love it.

Get her subscriptions to
her own magazines.

Remember, when she trusts her mother to stand by her in times of crisis, she'll learn to stand up for herself.

Watch that you don't start
using the word *we*, as in
"we are in cheerleading" or
"we are on the soccer team,"
or "we are in chorus."
It means "we" are going nuts.

Take her shopping for pretty, special-occasion outfits. Resist the urge for matching dresses.

Take her on hikes.
Explore ponds and meadows.
Sit outside under the stars
and point out constellations.
Develop her love of nature.

Teach her to write
thank-you notes.
For everything.

Make a tradition of mothers
and sisters and grandmothers all
dressing up and going to a fancy
tea once a year.

Help her enjoy being a young girl. There's plenty of time for her to be a young woman.

Teach her not to
exaggerate.

Realize that playing and talking
with your daughter are more
important than cleaning house
or making dinner.

Give her a bouquet of flowers at dance recitals, school plays, or after she places in the spelling bee.

Keep in mind that eleven-year-
old girls get extremely jealous.
Not only of other girls,
but of boys as well.

Realize that she'll gain confidence every time she does something outside her comfort zone. And succeeds.

Tell her the two of you may
disagree or even fight sometimes.
But you will always love her,
no matter what.

Enjoy every moment she wants to be around you. The clock is ticking.

The Awkward
Years

Realize one of life's cruelest ironies: Many girls go through puberty at about the same time their moms enter menopause.

Be prepared. The sweetest, gentlest fifth graders have been known to metamorphose into sullen, angry, nasty creatures who want nothing to do with their families.

Assure her it's okay that she's eight inches taller than the boys. They'll catch up.

Just accept that one
moment she'll be clingy,
the next moment she'll be
pushing you away.

Now you have someone
to enjoy chick flicks with.
Leave grumbling Dad
at home.

Encourage her to spend time with her grandmother. For some strange reason, they'll get along fine.

Teach her that perfume
shouldn't knock a family
out of their chairs
at breakfast.

Start a mother-daughter book club with other moms and daughters. Take turns picking books—remember, you have to read what she chooses too.

Give her a little rope.
Let her learn from her
mistakes while the stakes
aren't so high.

Accept that by the time she's in middle school she doesn't want you to know every thought in her head. And really, you don't want to know either.

Help her identify
her strengths.
And help her strengthen
her weaknesses.

Remind her that the "cookie-cutter" seventh and eighth graders on TV shows don't really exist.

Enforce three rules
early on: No eye rolling.
No door slamming.
Mutual respect.

Remind her to respect her teachers. They hold the key to a lot of awards, honors, and recommendations.

Spend your one-on-one
time doing not just
what interests you,
but her as well.

Understand that for girls,
independence usually starts
with hair. Ask yourself,
how important is it, really,
if it's blue?

You'll have moments when you feel like mom of the year. And moments when you're convinced you've failed her. In the same conversation.

Make sure she and Dad
spend time together.
They both need
each other.

Don't feel guilty about being the nosy mom who always checks to see if other adults are at home at her friends' houses. It'll keep her out of trouble.

Tell her
how well she's doing.

Remind her that neither
one of you is always right.
But you're always
the mom.

Have a girls' night with her
once a month—a night when
you paint toes, laugh, watch silly
TV shows, and have fun.

You'll worry about her not belonging. Ultimately, despite all your best help and support and advice, it's beyond your control.

Encourage her
to stand up to bullies.
Start early on this.

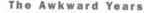
Teach her that the last
reason not to try
something is the fear she
may not do it well.

Ask her what color she'd
like for her bedroom.
Then spend the weekend
painting with her.

Don't let her moods
dominate the house.
Or else it will be one
insane house.

Don't wait for her grades to slip to become the homework police. Review her homework nightly.

Keep in mind that
a lot of girls today
have *too much* going on
outside school.

By middle school you can
tell what kind of brains
God gave your daughter.
And if she's using them.

Encourage her to do a little good every day.

Keep in mind,
even Mother Teresa
would be driven nuts by
a middle school daughter.

If she temporarily loses her spine, help her find it again.

Don't panic if she wants
to wear thong underwear
at thirteen.

Volunteer at her
school—chaperone a dance,
paint scenery for a play,
shelve books in the library.
It's a great way to participate
in your daughter's life.

Adolescent girls can be cruel. Be there for her when her feelings get hurt.

Let her have some control over the car radio, even if it hurts your ears. Try not to comment on her music. Really, really try.

Many former tomboys end up with "girlie" daughters, and vice versa. That's just how it goes.

Respect her privacy wishes.
Explain to her father why
his daughter needs to spend
ninety-seven hours holed up
in her room.

Remember, in even the healthiest mother-daughter relationships, rebellion sets in. Hug her, pray for her, wait for her to come back.

Remind her that girls who act dumb to attract boys attract dumb boys.

Remember, if a TV or computer isn't in her bedroom, she'll find it easier to study—and sleep.

There are advantages
to playing chauffeur:
Teenage girlfriends
talk nonstop in the backseat.
About everything.

When words utterly fail,
small, kind gestures like a
note or a funny card remind
her that Mom really cares.

Remember, a cell phone is a lifeline when you start dropping her off at the mall or concert or game.

Point out to her that truly smart girls listen more than they talk. But they also know when to speak up.

Don't carry grudges.
You're teaching her
to do the same.

Never make the mistake of thinking if you just do a little more for her, she'll magically become happy.

Teach her the art
of disagreeing without
being disagreeable.
It will take her far in life.

Understand that you can't know
enough about her at this age:
where she's going, who she's
going with, what they're doing,
who they're meeting, when
they'll be home.

Discipline with what's important
to her: the telephone, soccer,
dance, her friends. All's fair in
love and raising daughters.

Remember, how much she tells you is all about how you react. If you go nuclear and throw a tantrum over every little thing, she'll clam up.

Realize that everything in middle school is competition—friends, popularity, grades, clothes. She's under a lot of pressure.

Keep hugging her.

Participate together in a fund-raising walk for breast cancer research. Let her discover the power of thousands of women coming together for a cause.

Don't ever let her
believe that "Whatever"
is a conversation.

Don't forget, you are as big a mystery to her as she is to you.

A lot of girls find it safer to take their frustrations out on their mother. Tell her, ever so sweetly, you will have none of this.

Show her how to walk
in high heels without
tumbling over.

Take pictures even if she
whines, "Mom, don't!"
Later, she'll be glad
you did.

Insist she take part
in family traditions.
Happily.

Enforce your rules,
keep your standards high,
but keep telling her
you love her.

Remember, she needs a minimum eight hours' sleep. Impose a bedtime curfew.

Try to go for a day without criticizing or correcting her.

Get her involved in volunteer
work in your community.
The trick is to take her mind
off herself.

Accept that everything you do is going to embarrass your daughter. Especially being a good parent.

Every now and then, hold her hands, look her in the eye, and tell her she's the daughter you always wanted.

Girls
& Beauty

To some parents,
ChapStick is makeup. To others,
it's lipstick and nail polish.
You're the mom here.

Explain to her dad that most girls start getting their ears pierced around the age of ten. (He'll think twenty is more appropriate.)

Let her know
she doesn't need makeup
and highlighted hair
to be beautiful.

Allow her to wear what she feels great in. If there's nothing morally thorny about it, let it go even if it's not "your style."

Show her pictures of yourself when you had geeky glasses, bad hair, and horribly lame clothes. By her standards, anyway.

Give her the confidence
to wear what she wants
despite the dictates
of fashion.

Encourage her to
compliment other girls
on their clothes.
With sincerity.

If she doesn't see a problem with the length of her skirts or shorts, suggest she model them in front of her father.

Clue her in to the airbrushing techniques, plastic surgery, and makeup artists that enhance the "naturally" beautiful stars she sees in magazines.

Teach her that no shoe in
the world should require
a woman to have foot
surgery to wear it.

Show her how to dress like a million bucks with clothes from the sale rack. There will come a day when this is a life skill.

W hen your clothes start
disappearing, you'll be pleasantly
surprised that they were cool
enough to be borrowed.

Teach her that the real secrets
to fashion are posture and poise,
voice and speech, etiquette
and style. And these secrets
can be learned.

If her skin is a problem,
don't hesitate to get her
to a dermatologist.

Realize that no matter what your daughter wears, your husband will look at you and ask, "Do you think it's okay if she wears that?"

Be prepared: she will compare her clothes to the other girls'. She will want to blend in, not stand out.

Don't forget, her skin could break out, she might have to wear thick glasses, her hair could do weird things—but she still needs to think of herself as a beautiful person.

Make sure she understands never even to *experiment* with shoplifting. The number of girls who think they can get away with it is just stunning.

If need be, gently point out to her that wearing smaller sizes is not going to make her smaller.

To truly understand the generation gap, visit one of "her" stores. Moms have been known to experience visions in these places.

By eighth grade, she and her friends should be responsible enough to go shopping at the mall by themselves. As long as someone has a cell phone.

When she starts shopping without you, remind her that Mom reserves the final right of approval. Be ready to return a lot of stuff.

Accept that your daughter may be a born "fashionista" who has a better sense of style than you.

Remember, whenever there's a formal occasion, you'll be invited to go shopping. Have fun!

Consider giving her a credit
card to her favorite store, with
a monthly limit. Anything over
that she has to earn.

Remember,
the importance she attaches
to labels is directly proportional
to who's paying.

Explain that real beauty isn't about a skinny body or shiny hair. Being beautiful on the inside is what really matters.

When she tells you that your hair is cut wrong, your dresses are lame, and your shorts have got to go, it means she's trying to help you look sixteen. Resist.

Tell her it's okay to sometimes kick off her shoes and walk barefoot. Even in a prom dress.

Girls &
Other Girls

Remember, everything she learns about trusting women starts with you.

Teach her early on not to let other girls define who she is.

Remind her that making fun of her friends is a recipe for loneliness.

Encourage her to make friends at school, sports, church, the neighborhood . . . to have a wide range of friends from different backgrounds.

Remember, one of the hardest
things for a mom to watch
is when her daughter
is on the outs with her friends.

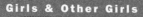
Explain to her that for a while, mean girls will be popular. But the mean girl should never be her.

If she's being ostracized, make a lot of time for her—on weekends, evenings, events, trips.

Explain to her father
that hiring a hit man
isn't an option.

Teach her that the girl who says,
"If you talk to *her*,
I won't be your friend,"
will never be a true friend.

Tell her about your high school reunion. That some of the happiest, most successful former classmates were basically unknowns in high school.

Teach her that a friend is somebody she can share her greatest successes with and who will be honestly happy for her.

Remind her that beauty, money,
or popularity doesn't
protect against meanness.
But kindness can overcome it.

Don't lose your marbles over mean girls and start calling moms, the principal, and the teachers. That's when your daughter quits talking to you.

Make your house the hangout house—filled with soft drinks and snacks and movies, where her friends are always welcome.

Teach her how to connect
with other women and
you've given her one of
life's great gifts.

Remember, she may not
want to talk to you,
but her friends often will.
Ask away.

Teach her that the really, really kind person is never forgotten.

Girls
& Boys

Tell her why you decided
to marry her father. Then
tell her the rest of the story.

Start discussions about your expectations, values, and morals early. If you wait till eighth grade, you've waited too long.

Keep in mind, there are actually
two major talks you'll
have with your daughter.
Before the "Boy Talk,"
there's the "What's Happening
to Your Body Talk."

She may bring up the "Boy Talk" anywhere. Like driving home from volleyball. Don't flinch.

Learn her lingo.
"Dating" a boy in middle school
might mean she talks to him
in science class.

Understand she has to get the facts from you. Girlfriends are just chock-full of misinformation.

Be aware that today's music, TV, magazines, and movies promote a hypersexual lifestyle. Make sure her values are not their values.

Remember,
boys show up at girls'
slumber parties.
Plan accordingly.

Keep in mind, only a fourteen-year-old girl could find anything remotely attractive about a fourteen-year-old boy.

Make sure she knows she can tell you anything. The less secrets at this age, the better.

Point out that if she wears clothes to draw boys' attention to her butt, attention will be drawn. Then what?

Don't stay up late
worrying that your
daughter doesn't have
a boyfriend. Get a life.

Teach her that no man
is worth betraying
another woman.

Remember, even if she's made a decision to delay sex, you need to keep talking to her about it.

Be careful about judging
a boy by his looks.
Learn something
about him first.

Teach her how to *expect* to be treated by a man. So she'll know when she's not being treated well and will refuse to tolerate it.

Tell her to find a boy who won't think a date to worship services is weird.

Warn her about the dangers of on-line "relationships." She should know never to give out real information or take anything at face value.

Don't push her
into a relationship just
so she can be popular.

In your sweetest voice, let her dates know it would be best for North America if your daughter were brought home on time, bright-eyed, and happy.

Don't fall "in love" with any of her boyfriends. Because she's not.

Encourage her to invite
her boyfriends over for
dinner.

Encourage her
not to kill chivalry
when she encounters it.

Tell her she needs to decide where her limits are before the heat of the moment. Because then there are no limits.

Explain that men will always feel they need to offer her advice. It's not their fault. They're genetically wired that way.

Stay out of her love life.
Never give a strange boy
your daughter's phone
number.

Remind her that
reputations are fragile.
And they follow you
around.

Keep Dad involved.
Don't hesitate to bring
him in when the issues
get more serious.

When a boy breaks her heart, curiously, you'll find yours in pieces too.

Girls & Extracurricular Activities

Develop her interest in sports early. Even if you never played anything. It will influence her physical, mental, and moral well-being the rest of her life.

Remember, everything is more competitive than when you were her age. Everything.

Encourage her to try a lot
of different activities. But don't
invest a ton of money in any
of them until she's ready to
make a commitment.

Practice soccer
or basketball
or softball with her.
Even if you're terrible.

Here's the deal about private lessons:

1. They cost a fortune.
2. Other girls are getting them.
3. Your daughter may quit in three years anyway.

Don't confuse your
dreams with hers.
Maybe she doesn't want
to be a cheerleader.

Coach her team if you know the game. Cheer on the sidelines if you don't.

Be a soccer mom.
It's a great life.

Remember, adolescent girls are defined by their activities: "She's in choir, she's a gymnast, she's an equestrian."

If you take her defeats
harder than she does,
you're not helping things.

Explain to her that Dad may suddenly be overcome by this urge to paint his stomach, his car, his face with her team colors. This is how men think.

Be calm about
all her tryouts.
She can't worry about
you *and* her performance.

Keep in mind,
tryouts for anything can be hard
on mothers and daughters.
And fathers. Even brothers.

Don't give her a speech when she loses. Give her a hug and a pizza.

It's perfectly normal to lie awake at 1 A.M. after she decides not to try out for the high school drill team despite ten years of private dance lessons and wonder, "What did we pay for?" You kept her active, graceful, and in good health.

Remember,
this is all extracurricular.
Grades come first.

Realize that competitive girls'
sports are cutthroat, vicious,
expensive, sometimes bloody,
and often humbling. Just like life.

Make sure her coaches
know what they're doing.
Then leave them alone.

Teach her
to win honorably.
And to lose with grace.

Girls &
Money

In spite of what she tells you, all she really needs is food and clothing and shelter and love. The rest is gravy.

Teach her to budget her
spending. Even when her
allowance is only a couple
of dollars a week.

Remind her she's
been blessed by God.
And she must give
something back.

Explain that if she ever loans money to a friend, she could wind up losing both.

Challenge her to figure out tips in restaurants, sales tax in stores, and percentage reductions to hone her math and money skills.

Teach her to shop the sales.

Show her how to
negotiate . . . for a car,
a raise, a discount,
a home.

Encourage her to find a summer job that matches her interests, whether it's working at an animal shelter, day camp, or clothing store. She'll earn money *and* real experience.

Review with her the costs
of college and the impact of
scholarships and financial aid
in light of your family's own
financial situation.

Teach her to always carry
a zero balance on all her
credit cards.

Give her money smarts.
Explain how to balance a
checkbook, the dangers of
spending more than you make,
the importance of saving.

If she says all her friends
are carrying $450 purses and she
wants one too, smile, hug her,
and hand her the want ads.

Remind her to spend less than she could. And to give back more than she should.

Help her invest in a mutual fund when she's in high school. She's never too young to start financial planning.

Teach her never to be
afraid to face and
deal with financial fears.

Girls & Success

Remember, girls whose parents have high expectations for them also have high expectations for themselves. It just works out that way.

Work with her
on her study skills.
How else will she learn?

Help her understand what it means to be successful. You and your daughter should both know the answer . . . in detail.

Keep in mind that you can only provide her with opportunity. The rest is up to her.

Remind her that the path to success often requires a teammate.

Never let her forget
that the only thing
she can control in this life
is her mind.

Help her learn the
art of conversation.
It will take her
everywhere in life.

Talk to her about first impressions—ones she's had about other people, and the impressions people will have about her.

Never take credit for her successes. Or the blame for her failures.

Give her responsibility
before she reaches adulthood.
She'll make mistakes, of course,
but there will also be times
she'll really impress you.

Teach her that
enthusiasm is one of life's
greatest gifts . . . and that
it can be learned.

Let her know
she can be successful
while still being kind
and considerate.

Remember, some of the most successful people in the world just had to deal with setbacks because self-indulgence was an option they could not afford.

Teach her the healthiest women are the ones who are independent.

There will be times when she says life is unfair. Explain to her it was never a given that life is fair.

Show her how to
ask for what she wants.
Then to accept the
outcome.

Inevitably, games will be lost, elections will go the wrong way. Don't encourage her to quit when the going gets hard. Encourage her to develop some muscle.

Tell her it's the end
result that matters.
Not where you start.

When she's older,
remind her that young
girls now look up to *her*
as a role model.

Never forget,
the greatest barrier to
her success could be too
much criticism from you.

Teach her that willingness to accept responsibility for one's own life is what separates the women from the girls.

Girls &
Spirituality

Tell her that
God created her as an
answer to your prayers.

Encourage her to make choices wisely. Because even the smallest decisions can have the biggest consequences.

Teach her to find
ten blessings a day.
Twenty on bad days.

Stress God early in her life. Don't wait until high school and she's in trouble to insist she go to church or synagogue every week.

Teach her to talk to God
throughout the day,
when things get rough
and when things go well.

Never forget that
you can't teach your daughter
about God if you don't have
a relationship with Him.

Remember, teaching her about
God is not unlike teaching her
about sex. It's not all at once—it's
the way you live your life every day.

Share your most mystical
experience with her.
Over and over again.

Don't let her turn her
back on life's blessings.
Teach her to stay
the course.

Teach her God gives us
all different gifts.
It's how we use them
that matters.

Let her see you give of yourself unselfishly. Not just your money, but your time, your patience, and your love.

Encourage her
to pray for the people she
doesn't get along with.
One day it could be you.

Fill your house with warmth, love, and joy, and you'll find it's also filled with her and her friends.

Tell her some of life's
most puzzling questions
have no simple answers.

You will have to remind her God has a plan. And maybe it's not for her to be a model, but something even more special.

Older Girls

Be prepared, not just for new boys she brings home in high school, but for new girls too. You might easily prefer the boys.

Smother her with love.
Not advice.

Don't give her rope to mope around the house. Get her up, push her out into the world.

Keep your chin up.
Your real daughter
will come back.

Teach her to respond to insults with class.

Discuss the nonnegotiables about driving: the seat belt, the speed limit, zero tolerance for alcohol and, if she's driving your car, anything looking like a garter hanging from the mirror.

Show her how to fill a gas tank
without getting gas on her shoes.

Remind her when necessary that reckless adolescent behavior will lead to a permanently parked car.

Teach her never to get into a car with a drunk girl or boy. That she can always call you to pick her up, no questions asked.

Realize some girls don't know when they're being drama queens and when they're truly distraught. But wise moms do.

Remember, there may come a time in high school when she won't understand why she can't stay out till 2 A.M., date a gangster, study only one hour a week, or live apart from the family.

Do not fall into the
"I just want her to be happy" trap.
Happiness for her is probably
skipping school and
driving a Beemer at sixteen.

Introduce your daughter to a gynecologist when she turns sixteen. Tell her she's free to find her own as long as she keeps regular appointments.

Instead of starting
World War III over her room,
just tell her no more new clothes
until she picks up what
she already owns for
three months straight.

Teach her how to change a tire, to use an electric drill, to mow the lawn. She should never have to depend on some guy to do it for her.

Join a women-friendly gym together. You could probably use the exercise, and she could use the one-on-one time.

Those problems
she's telling you about?
The best way to help her
is to just listen.

Use the things she tells you in confidence against her and you've committed the ultimate betrayal.

Challenge her to take the honors and advanced placement classes her school offers. Don't let her just coast along.

On the other hand, she may be smart enough to handle five AP courses, but she may not have the time or strength. Help her to understand her limits.

Never forget,
a confident daughter
will always know
her mother's reaction.

Remind her that if she doesn't feel good about herself, no one else around her is going to feel good about her either.

Show her how to recognize
dangerous situations . . .
if she feels her heart racing,
it's time to get out of there.

Give her options
she can use to get out
of bad situations.
Review them regularly.

As difficult as it may be,
accept her apologies.
With affection.

Recognize that for all her pulling away and moods and arguments and words, there will be times when she wants nothing more than to talk to her mother.

Sometimes,
all you can do is be there.
Without words.

Give her a budget for her prom dresses and shoes and dinners and limos and after-parties. Make it lower than your house payment.

Realize that if you still want to be involved in every aspect of her life, you really don't have enough to do.

Tell her it's a good idea
to make friends
with people smarter
than she is.

Remember, a time will come when you will say, "*You* figure it out." It will be hard on both of you.

Encourage her to travel.

Give her the great
books you want her to
read someday.

Caution her about hanging around people who like to just "kill time." That phrase says it all.

Tell her to be careful about who she reveals her personal life to.

Take heart in knowing you might actually talk to her more often on the phone when she's away at college than you did when she lived under your roof.

Tell her if at first she doesn't succeed, do it the way Mom would have told her to do it in the first place.

Encourage her to settle
her arguments in minutes.
Not hang on to them
for weeks.

If she's trying to choose between a boyfriend and a scholarship, insist she take the scholarship.

Tell her not to worry about being better than a man. Just be better as a woman.

Remind her that life is nothing if not a daring adventure.

Send her out into
the world prepared . . .
with her grandmothers'
recipe books.

Remind her over and over again: It's all about who her friends are.

Realize sometimes she just can't say or show that she loves you. But she does.

Caution her before she gives up her dreams for any job. Or any man.

Remember,
even the oldest women
need their mothers
sometimes.

Don't be jealous
of her other mentors.
Be grateful.

Resolve you won't make
her feel guilty about not calling
or coming over more often
after she leaves home.

Tell her how much joy
she's brought into
your life.

And in the end,

L et her go.